Looking at Insects

David Suzuki

with BARBARA HEHNER

Stoddart Young Readers

First published in 1986 by
Stoddart Publishing Co. Limited
34 Lesmill Road
Toronto, Canada
M3B 2T6

First printing, February 1986
Second printing, May 1986

CANADIAN CATALOGUING IN PUBLICATION DATA

Suzuki, David T., 1936-
  David Suzuki: looking at insects

Includes index.
ISBN 0-7737-5062-2

1. Insects — Juvenile literature.   I. Hehner, Barbara, 1947-   II. Title.

QL467.2.S95 1986   j595.7   C86-093157-9

ILLUSTRATIONS © 1986 by R. Tuckerman
DESIGN: Brant Cowie/Artplus
COVER PHOTOGRAPH: Peter Paterson
TYPESETTING: Jay Tee Graphics Ltd.

Printed in Canada

Table of Contents

To Alice and Chet Embury, with love
and
In memory of Setsu Nakamura Suzuki

The writing of this book was aided in part by Public Awareness Program for Science and Technology Grant GP85-00012. The authors would also like to thank Dr. Stephen Tobe, of the Department of Zoology, University of Toronto, for his helpful comments on the manuscript.

AN IMPORTANT NOTE FOR KIDS AND GROWNUPS
You will see this ⊘ warning sign on some of the **Things to Do** in this book. It means that an adult should help out. The project may use some boiling water or something might need to be cut with a knife. Everyone needs to be extra careful. Most grownups will want to get involved in these nature projects anyway — why should kids have all the fun?

Introduction

When I say "Nature," what do you think about? Probably trees, fish, birds and mammals — big things that are easily seen. But nature is full of smaller creatures that are every bit as varied and interesting — the world of *insects*. Even in the middle of a large city, you can find all kinds of insects. From beautiful butterflies and moths to hard-working honeybees and ants to pesky flies and mosquitoes, insects are an important part of the world around us.

To really appreciate insects, try to imagine what it would be like if we were shrunk down to the size of a ladybug. Now blades of grass would seem like giant trees. Everywhere there would be huge birds, spiders and other animals trying to eat us. How would we travel and find food, where would we live, and how could we find each other? Now I think you can see why insects are interesting.

As far back as I can remember, I collected insects. I used to have jars and cans full of them. Luckily for me, my mom and dad encouraged me instead of tossing them out. Even now, I find I can sit and watch ants for hours. So I'm always surprised when people screw up their faces and say, "Insects! Yuk! Take them away!" That's because they think of insects as creepie-crawlies and they don't like them. I hope that after you have read this book and met a few insects, you'll agree that they are wonderful and fascinating friends.

DAVID SUZUKI

The World of Insects

A Small, Strange World

Suppose you have travelled far, far back in time — to the world as it was 300 million years ago. You find it very warm and humid. A lot of the land is swampy. You can't see any trees, but you can see lots of giant ferns.

What is that winging its way toward you? It's a dragonfly — but it's as big as a seagull! You can't help ducking as it flies over. But there aren't any other people around to be startled by this dragonfly. The first human-like creatures didn't appear until much, much later. Insects have been around more than 300 times as long as we have!

Now travel back to the present, and make a landing right in your own backyard. It may look pretty peaceful on a summer afternoon. But if you really look closely, there's an amazing, busy world to see. Insects are all around you — crawling in the grass, burrowing under stones, buzzing and fluttering in the air. They're taking their first flights, building underground cities, and fighting fierce battles. None of them is anywhere near as big as that prehistoric dragonfly, so it's easy to forget that they are everywhere.

In about one square metre (one square yard) of your backyard, there are probably between 500 and 2,000 insects. In a couple of square kilometres (a little over a square mile) of parkland, there are probably more insects than there are people in the whole world!

Insects can live just about anywhere — on land, in trees, underground, in fresh water and salty water, in ice and snow, and in pools of oil. Some of them spend their lives riding around on other animals, or even living inside them. Insects can eat almost anything. Some eat meat, some eat fruits and vegetables. Some drink the juice of flowers and some drink your blood. There are even insects that eat wood.

People who study insects have found more than a million different kinds. Each year, they discover many thousands of new kinds — and there are many more still to be discovered. Insects can be any color you can imagine. They can be as skinny as twigs, big and fuzzy, or shiny and hard. No matter how different from each other these creatures seem, they're all insects. They all have the same basic body parts. They all have a head, a midsection called a *thorax*, and an end part called an *abdomen*.

All insects have six legs, which are attached to the thorax. How do you think you would move six legs? One at a time? One pair at a time? Here is what many insects do. They move the front right leg and the back right leg at the same time as the middle *left* leg. Then they put those down and pick up the front left leg, the back left leg and the middle *right* leg. Got it now? Maybe you're glad you just have two legs to worry about!

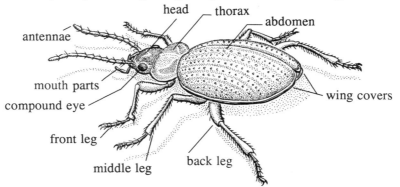

Many adult insects also have one or two pairs of wings attached to their thorax.

Have you ever seen a fly or a bee fly right into a wall or a window and then, buzzing furiously, take off in another direction? If you ran into a wall, you might be very badly hurt. Why aren't insects? Well, it's because they wear suits of armor. Instead of having their bones inside their bodies as we do, insects have a hard outer shell called an *exoskeleton*. (*Exo* comes from the Greek word for "outside.")

Inside, insects are very different from you, too. Although they breathe air, they don't have any lungs. They breathe through little tubes that open along the sides of their bodies. They don't have blood vessels, either. Their blood travels freely through their bodies. It can be yellow or green, but it's not usually red. That red blood you see when you squash a mosquito is probably yours!

Let's start looking at that strange small world that's all around us. Who knows what adventures we're about to see?

How to Capture Insects Without Hurting Them

Most insects are not dangerous for you to handle. In fact, *they're* the ones who are in danger from *you*, unless you know how to treat them gently.

What You Need:

a clear plastic drinking glass
a piece of cardboard

What to Do:

I. How to Capture Flying Insects

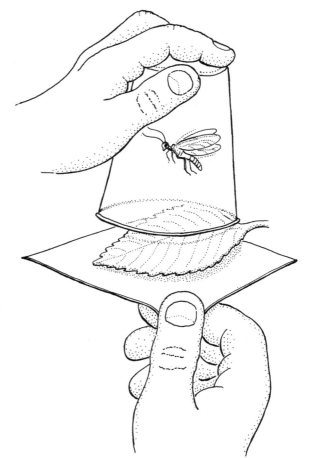

1. Wait until an insect is busy drinking nectar or sitting quietly on a leaf. Hold the glass upside down over the flower or leaf. As the insect becomes aware of danger, it will fly upward. Quickly slip the piece of cardboard across the rim of the glass.

2. Holding the cardboard in place, carry the insect to a table. Set down the glass. Now you can have a good look at your captive through the sides of the glass.

II. How to Capture Green Lacewings

1. Lacewings can be found on a summer night on screen doors and windows. They have very long wings that stick out past their bodies. You can pick them up by clamping your thumb and forefinger — *carefully!* — on the outer tips of the wings. Carry the insect to your insect cage. (You will learn how to make an insect cage on page 13.)

   You can also use the glass and cardboard method for lacewings.

III. How to Capture Ladybugs

1. Moisten the tip of your finger. *Gently* lay your finger on the ladybug's back. The ladybug will stick to your finger long enough for you to put it in your insect cage.

IV. How to Capture Ants and Other Crawling Insects

1. Lay a small piece of paper or cardboard across the insect's path. Cover the insect with the clear plastic glass. Be careful not to injure any of its legs with the edge of the glass. Carry it to a table where you can have a closer look at it.

V. Insects that Should Not Be Captured:

1. Bees and wasps — Don't take a chance on being stung. Just watch them outside from a safe distance.
2. Dragonflies — They are very hard to catch, unless you have a net. Even with a net, it takes great skill to catch a dragonfly without hurting it. Just watch them outdoors.
3. Don't capture water beetles and ground beetles with your hands. Some of them can give a painful bite.

SOMETHING TO DO

A Magnifying Insect Cage

Sometimes it's handy to have an insect cage so that you can spend some time looking closely at an insect before you let it go. Here, and on page 15, you'll learn how to make two easy cages.

What You Need:

a clear plastic drinking glass,
    made of soft plastic
a magnifying glass with a
    diameter of about 8 cm (3 in.)
scissors
tape measure or ruler
cloth tape

What to Do:

1. First, test your magnifying glass. Find out how far away from an object you need to hold it, so that you can see the object clearly. Use a tape measure or ruler to measure the distance.
2. Measure the same distance on the plastic glass, starting from the rim.
3. ⊘ Cut away the bottom part of the plastic glass with scissors. Now you have a plastic tube open at both ends.

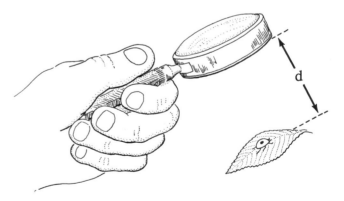

4. Put the magnifying glass on one of the open ends of the plastic glass. Choose the end on which the magnifying glass fits best. Use tape to attach the magnifying glass to the plastic.

5. Now you have a magnifying insect cage. Through its sides, you can see the insect life-size. Through the magnifying glass on top, you can see details of the insect.

6. Capture an insect gently (see page 11) and put it in the cage. When you've finished looking at it, let it go.

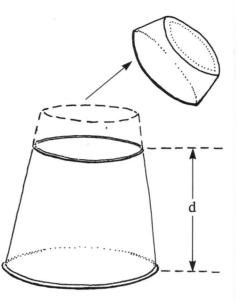

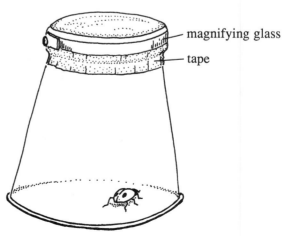

magnifying glass

tape

Insects to Go

This is a handy insect cage that you can take with you on a nature walk.

What You Need:

a piece of small gauge wire
   screen, about 20 cm by 20 cm
   (7 in. square) — you can get
   this at a hardware store
small pieces of wire or twist ties
   from sandwich bags
adhesive tape
lids from large spray cans
   (hairspray, laundry starch,
   carpet cleaner, etc.)
a long pipe cleaner

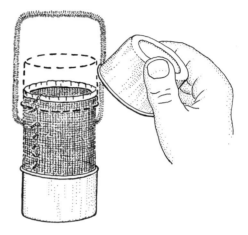

What to Do:

1. ⊘ Roll the wire screen into a
   tube so that it just fits into
   one of the lids. Wire the
   edges of the tube together
   with small pieces of wire or
   twist ties.
2. ⊘ Wrap any rough edges of
   wire with adhesive tape so
   that you won't be scratched.
3. Place the wire tube in one of
   the lids. The open end will be
   the top of your insect cage.
   Attach the pipe cleaner to the
   wire so that it makes a curved
   handle over the top of the
   cage. Remember to leave
   enough room to fit on the top
   lid.
4. Put on the top lid and take
   your travelling insect cage for
   a walk. You can keep insects
   in this cage for a short time
   while you have a good look at
   them or show them to your
   friends. Then let them go.

An Instant Insect Collection

You probably have an interesting insect collection right in your own house. You don't think so? Let's start looking. Even if you're a person who gets a little scared handling live insects, you may find it fun to look at some dead ones.

What You Need:

a cardboard box
a magnifying glass
some modelling clay
some straight pins

What to Do:

1. Look on window sills or between the windows and the screens. Chances are you'll find some dead insects there. What position do you usually find dead insects in? Put them in your cardboard box. Handle them carefully — they may break easily.
2. ⊘ Light fixtures that haven't been cleaned for a while often have insects in them. Ceiling lights usually have the best collections. Ask an adult to help you unscrew the lamp shade. Then you can dump your finds into your cardboard box.
3. You may find an especially interesting kind of dead insect in spider webs. Some spiders wrap their prey in spider silk so that they look like little mummies. If you unwrap the

threads very carefully, you will find an insect body inside. Spiders suck the juices out of their prey, so you may find just the outer shell of the insect.

4. How many different kinds of insects have you found? Have you found things that *aren't* insects? How do you know? Get an insect book from the library to find the names of the insects in your collection. Have a look at the insects through your magnifying glass.

5. You might like to mount a couple of the insects you find. (This will *not* work with very dry insects that have been lying around for a while.) Here's how to do it. Stick a straight pin into the underside of the insect. Make a little ball of modelling clay. Put the head of the pin in the clay. Press the clay onto a small piece of cardboard. Write the name of the insect on the piece of cardboard.

6. Wash your hands when you're finished handling your insects!

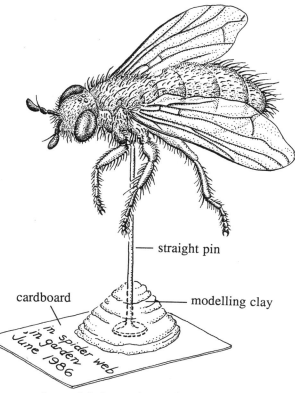

straight pin

cardboard

modelling clay

in spider web
in garden
June 1986

always label your insects!

The World's Longest Insect

Can you imagine an insect almost twice as long as an unsharpened pencil? The bodies of the giant stick insects of Indonesia are about 33 cm (13 inches) long. A brand-new pencil is only about 19 cm (7½ inches) long.

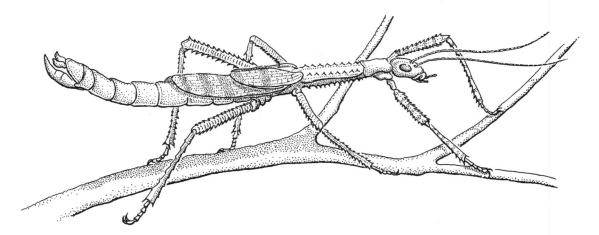

Olympic High Jumpers — Insect Division

Who do you think are the best insect leapers? Most people would probably guess grasshoppers. For their size, though, fleas are the champs. That's right, those pesky little critters that live on dogs and cats — and lots of other animals — and bite them. A flea can jump about 20 cm (8 inches) in the air. This may not sound like much. But a flea is only about 2 mm (less than 1/10th of an inch) long, so it is jumping 100 times its length. If a person could leap that high, he or she could jump over a 40-storey building in a single bound!

Have You Ever Met a Morphosis?

*H*ave you ever heard someone say that cats have nine lives? It's not really true, of course. People say this because cats sometimes seem able to live through falls and accidents that would kill other creatures. However, we could truthfully say that mammals have *two* life stages. (Mammals are the animals that give birth to live young — instead of laying eggs — and feed their young milk. Cats are mammals, and so are human beings.)

In the first part of your life, you floated around in liquid inside your mother's body — but you didn't drown. By the time you were born, you had grown into a full-sized baby able to live outside your mother's body and breathe air. When you were born, your "second life" began.

Most insects go through a lot more changes than we do — they have *four* stages in their lives. We call the changes that they go through *metamorphosis.* An insect may look so different in each stage of its life that you can't tell it's the same creature.

Nearly all insects begin as tiny *eggs* laid by the female insect. Insects can lay hundreds of eggs at a time. What do you think hatches out of these eggs? Not baby-sized insects, as you might expect. Instead, they are little worm-like things called *larvae.* (One of them is called a *larva.*)

Larvae look so different from adult insects that we often have special names for them. *Maggots,* which you may see on dead animals or

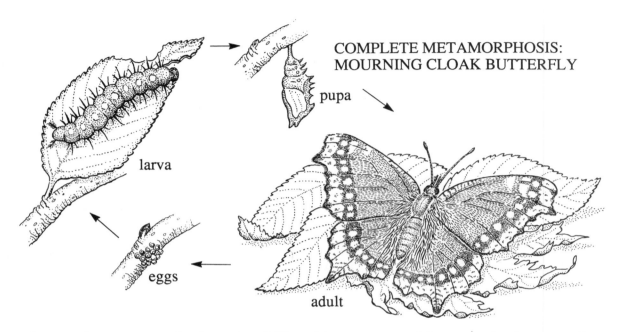

COMPLETE METAMORPHOSIS:
MOURNING CLOAK BUTTERFLY

pupa

larva

eggs

adult

decayed meat, are the larvae of flies. Fuzzy *caterpillars* are the larvae of butterflies and moths.

Larvae have just one job in life: to eat and eat and eat. As you would expect, they grow very quickly. But how do you grow when your skeleton is on the outside? You can't. Instead, the larval shell splits down the back and the larva wiggles out. After a few hours, its outside has hardened into a new and larger exoskeleton. Larvae go through this many times before they finish growing.

What's the next stage in an insect's life adventure? It becomes a *pupa*. Pupa is the Latin word for *doll*. And pupae do look like little dolls all wrapped up in blankets. Some of them — including moth larvae — wrap themselves in silk cocoons.

Inside its shell, the whole larva breaks down into mush. Then it does an amazing thing. It rebuilds itself into an adult insect. This adult insect

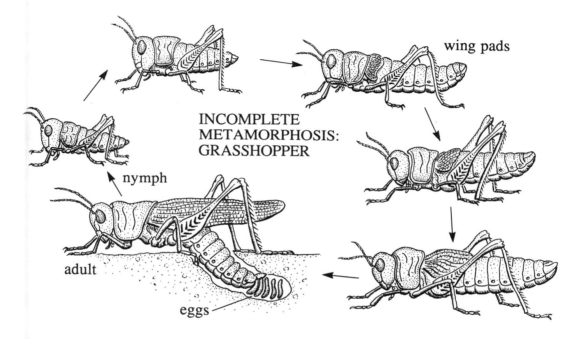

INCOMPLETE
METAMORPHOSIS:
GRASSHOPPER

wing pads

nymph

adult

eggs

looks nothing like the larva who entered the pupal stage. After a few weeks or months, when the weather is just right, the insect breaks out of the pupa's outer shell. Then it begins its fourth and final life.

A few insects — including grasshoppers and dragonflies — don't go through all these stages. They have an *incomplete metamorphosis.* Young insects hatch from their eggs looking something like the adults they will be. These young insects are called *nymphs.* Grasshopper nymphs have no wings. As they grow and shed their outer coats, the wings appear little by little.

Why do insects go through all these changes? Insects are the food for many other animals, including other insects. When they start off as tiny eggs instead of live babies, they can start off in huge numbers. Even if many are eaten before they reach adult life, some will survive.

Often larvae and nymphs eat different food from their parents. Dragonfly nymphs have gills and can breathe underwater. They catch their food there. Fully grown dragonflies live in the air and catch other winged insects. This means that parents and offspring don't have to compete for food, even if they live near each other.

Insects *specialize* in different things at different times of their lives. Larvae don't move around much; they just eat. When it gets cold and food is scarce, they become pupae. Pupae don't need to eat. Many adult insects don't need to eat much either. They stored up food in their bodies while they were larvae.

Many adult insects have wings, so they can fly around looking for a mate. Then the females can search for the very best place to lay their eggs. And it all begins again.

Mothering Some Mealworms

Mealworms aren't really worms at all — they're the larvae of little black beetles. They're sold in pet stores as food for pet frogs and snakes, but if you feed the mealworms instead, you can watch a complete insect life cycle.

What You Need:

2 or 3 dozen mealworms
  (sometimes you can find
  some in old flour that's
  been kept too long — or you
  can get them at a pet store)
a rectangular food storage box
  made of soft plastic, and its
  lid
window screen
freezer tape
scissors
rolled oats
sliced apple or potato
a piece of burlap or other loose-
  woven cloth, cut to fit box

mealworms will be able to get some air.

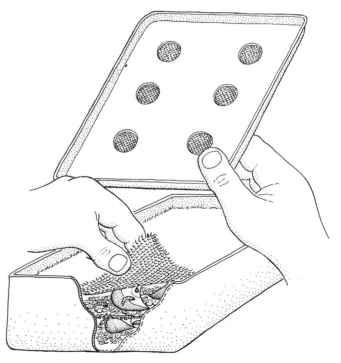

What to Do:

1. ⊘ Cut five or six holes in the lid of the box, so that the

2. ⊘ Cut small pieces of window screen to fit over the holes. Tape them in place, using the freezer tape.
3. In the box, make layers of food, mealworms and burlap. Start by putting some oats in the box, about 1 cm (¼ in.) deep. Then place a couple of thin slices of potato or apple on the oatmeal. Next put about a dozen mealworms in the box. Cover them with a piece of burlap. Repeat the layers until the box is full or you run out of mealworms.
4. Put the lid on the box. Keep it at room temperature. After a few days, the larvae (mealworms) you put in the box will become pupae. In a couple of weeks, adult beetles will appear. Where did they come from? The adult beetles will lay eggs between the layers of burlap. What do you think will come out of the eggs?
5. You can keep this mealworm farm going for about a month. Then it's time to clean the box and restock it with fresh food.

MEALWORM LIFE STAGES

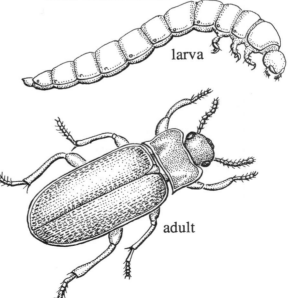

larva

adult

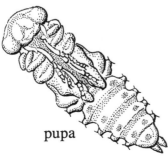

pupa

Just Suppose

Suppose a single pair of houseflies mates in April. The female lays some eggs. Suppose all the eggs hatch into larvae. Suppose all the larvae survive to become adult flies, who mate and lay eggs. Suppose this goes on all summer. How many flies could that single April pair produce? 190,000,000,000,000,000,000! They would cover the whole earth about 14 m (47 feet) deep.

This doesn't happen, of course. All over the world, people are swatting flies and spraying poisons on them. Birds and other animals are eating them. Millions and millions are killed. But you can see why the housefly has always been a pesky houseguest.

An Insect Horror Story

The mother dauber wasp works hard to shape a mud nest for her eggs. Then she goes hunting for a fat juicy spider. When she finds it, she paralyses it by stinging it. She hauls the spider back to her nest. The spider is still alive but it can't move a muscle. The mother dauber wasp seals the nest, with her eggs and the spider inside. Then she flies away. When the wasp larvae hatch, a meal is waiting for them. The larvae start eating the least important parts of the spider first. This way, the spider stays alive until the very end, when its vital organs are eaten. Ugh — it sounds pretty cruel, doesn't it? But most insects — and spiders too — have no choice; they have to kill other creatures to stay alive themselves. And dauber wasps have no refrigerators. This is the only way they can give their larvae fresh meat.

Tell An Insect's Life Story

What do you think a caterpillar feels like when its skin is too tight? Do you think it gets itchy and restless? What do you think a butterfly feels like when it first discovers it can fly? You might like to write a story or draw a cartoon strip about an insect going through its four "lives." What adventures and close escapes did it have? Which stage of life did it like best? Why?

How Insects Defend Themselves

Have you ever watched bats at night zipping through the air? They are catching a lot of insects. Have you ever watched fish jumping in a lake? They're after insects, too. Insects are breakfast, lunch and dinner to a lot of creatures, so they have developed ways to protect themselves from being eaten. Here are a few of them.

Insects have a coat of armor, their tough outer surface, but they also have weapons. Some caterpillars are covered in beautiful hair, but the hairs are like needles tipped with irritating chemicals. So be careful when you pick one up. Stag beetles have giant jaws to fight off attackers. And we all know that bees, wasps and hornets have stingers that can be very painful. Remember, they only sting when they are threatened. Probably, the best way to keep out of trouble is to get away fast. That's exactly what grasshoppers do, with their strong legs for jumping.

Let's go back to the bats. They find insects by giving high-pitched squeaks. Then they listen for the echo of that sound bouncing off an insect. (That's how submarines and whales can tell if there's anything ahead.) Well, some moths have developed a defence. When they hear the bat's squeaks, they go into a dive. Then they flutter in a crooked flight that makes them hard to catch. And a lot of them get away!

Long ago, insects discovered chemical warfare. The bombardier beetle has a special chamber inside its body. It turns its rear end towards its enemies while special chemicals are mixed in the chamber. A chemical reaction builds up the temperature until it explodes with a hot squirt of burning, itching juices. You can imagine what a shock a mouse or a bird gets when it tries to eat a bombardier beetle!

Have you ever picked up a stink bug? You can recognize it by its shield-like shape. If you smell your fingers after holding one — peeuw! They sure are named right! The stink bug releases a terrible smell to discourage anything that might want to eat it.

Milkweed plants are poisonous to most living things. But monarch butterfly caterpillars eat milkweed leaves and store the poisonous chemicals in their bodies. An unknowing bird may see the brightly colored monarch caterpillar or butterfly and catch it. But soon after it eats the insect, the bird will get very sick. Birds quickly learn to leave monarchs alone. Now the interesting thing is that a completely different kind of butterfly, the viceroy, looks very similar to the monarch. It doesn't live on milkweed, and it is good to eat. But because birds have learned that monarchs taste awful, they avoid the viceroy, too. The viceroy has a better chance of living, thanks to the monarch.

Other insects defend themselves by fading into the background — they use *camouflage*. The walking stick is a familiar example. Its body looks like a twig and its legs look like branches. You have to look very carefully to see it. Many insects look like leaves. The katydid looks like a bright green leaf, complete with veins, while the kallima butterfly of India looks like a dead leaf. A tree hopper has a huge spike sticking up from its back that makes it look just like a thorn.

So these small creatures have come up with ingenious ways to avoid their enemies. And it has worked.

SOMETHING TO DO

Now You See Them — Now You Don't

Insects hide from their enemies by being hard to see. They may be the same color as their favorite leaves or bark. This is called *camouflage*. Does it really work?

What You Need:

an area of lawn
measuring tape
a ball of string
some small sticks

toothpicks in several colors
a partner
a watch

What To Do:

1. Use the tape measure to measure a piece of lawn about 2 m by 1 m (6 ft. by 3 ft.). Put sticks in the corners and once or twice along the sides. Run a piece of string around the sticks to mark off the area.

2. Count out 20 toothpicks in each of four or five colors. Include green, natural wood color and red in your colors. Ask your partner to scatter the toothpicks on the grass.

3. Now have your partner count off 10 seconds while you try to pick up as many red toothpicks as you can. How many did you get? Next see how many green toothpicks you can pick up. Repeat this for all the colors. You could make a chart similar to the one on page 30 to show how you did.

   Now you scatter the toothpicks. Let your partner try picking them up.

4. Which toothpicks were the hardest to find? Which were the easiest? What does this show you about the way insects hide from their enemies?

	1-5 toothpicks	6-10 toothpicks	11-15 toothpicks	16-20 toothpicks
Red				
Green				
Yellow				
Pink				
White				
Natural Wood				

The Hoverfly Mistake

Hoverflies have only one defence — they look like bees. Like bees, they visit flowers to drink nectar, and like bees, they are striped yellow and black. Birds don't try to eat them because they don't want to be stung. The hoverflies' disguise led to a strange belief that lasted for hundreds of years. Ancient Greek and Roman scholars wrote that if you left an animal's body to rot, it would produce bees. Until the seventeenth century, this was thought to be the way bees were born. It's pretty certain that what people saw were hoverflies. Like other flies, they lay their eggs on rotting things. No matter how long people waited, these "bees" never made a drop of honey for them!

HOVERFLY

HONEYBEE

The Moths That Were Changed By Smoke

About 150 years ago, peppered moths fluttered around the English countryside. They had white wings with little black speckles like pepper. When they rested on light-colored tree trunks, hungry birds couldn't see them. Every once in a while, a darker-colored moth was born. But it could not hide on the light bark and the birds could see it and eat it.

Then, in the part of England where the peppered moths lived, many factories were built. The factories filled the air with black smoke. The tree trunks became dark with soot. Now the white moths were easy for the birds to see. They were quickly gobbled up. But the dark moths could hide so more of them lived to lay eggs and have offspring. Today, almost all the peppered moths are a dark sooty brown. This gradual change in how a kind of animal looks is called *evolution*.

How Insects See And Sense Things

I can smell without a nose,
I can sing without a voice,
I hear with my knees.
What am I?

The answer to this riddle is *an insect*. Just like you, an insect needs its senses to survive. But its eyes, ears and other sense organs are very different from yours.

You have to turn your head to look both ways before you cross the street. But a fly can see in all directions at once with its big, bulging eyes. If you've ever tried to catch or swat a fly, you know how well its eyesight protects it from danger. Dragonflies, which hunt other insects while they fly through the air, also have very large eyes and keen eyesight.

Insect eyes are nothing like your eyes. Insects have *compound eyes*. They're made up of hundreds — even thousands — of small, six-sided eyes. It's almost impossible for us to imagine how the world looks through these eyes. (The drawing on page 34 shows a section of the compound eye removed to show how each eye is made up of many smaller eyes.)

Talking is very important to human beings. It is the main way we share news and ideas. Insects need to communicate, too. One way is by sound, but they have no vocal chords. Some of them can make loud noises with other parts of their bodies. Crickets make their cheerful chirping by rubbing one rough wing over the other. Grasshoppers make their sawing sounds by rubbing their legs against their abdomens or their wings. Cicadas have pieces of skin on their thoraxes that can vibrate (shake very fast) to make a loud noise. All these insect musicians are males. Their songs are saying "Here I am. I'm looking for a mate." If the males stay in one spot, the females will soon find them.

COMPOUND EYE AND ANTENNAE

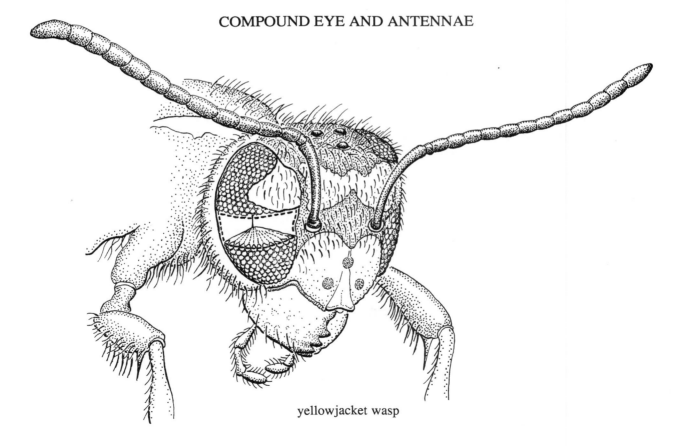

yellowjacket wasp

In order to hear the singing, insects have to have "ears". But they're not where you'd expect to find them. Crickets and some kinds of grasshoppers hear through holes on their front legs. Cicadas have ears on their abdomens!

Noisemakers and ears make it easier for some insects to find mates. But what do the rest of them do? For many kinds of insects, eyes don't help much. If you think about how tiny insects are, you'll understand why. A small patch of grass is like a forest of giant trees. Mates are very hard to see. Often they're even the same color as the grass. Besides, many insects are only active at night, when it's too dark to spot a mate.

Insects get around this problem by using their sense of smell. They give off special chemicals called *pheromones*. Other animals can't smell them, but the insects can. A male moth can find a female moth who is *several kilometres* away by following her scent. Insects pick up smells with two very sensitive organs called *antennae*. Antennae are found on insects' heads. Some are feathery, some are twisted around and around like a telephone cord, some are cone-shaped. All of them are very important for smelling — and tasting and touching, too.

Most insects live their lives alone, except at mating time. A few kinds, including ants and termites, live in big groups. It's too dark inside their nests to use their eyes. In fact, some termites and ants are blind. They use their antennae to follow each other along a trail to food, to tell the difference between friends and enemies, and to warn each other of danger. You might not enjoy your food so much if you lost your sense of smell, but your day-to-day life wouldn't change. However, without a sense of smell, an insect can't survive.

SOMETHING TO DO

Listening In On An Insect

What You Need:

a paper cup
a piece of wax paper
an elastic band
a flying insect

What To Do:

1. Capture a flying insect with your paper cup. Here's the easiest way to do it. Choose an insect that is resting on a flat surface such as a window. Quickly put the cup over the insect so that it is trapped between the cup and the window.
2. Slide your piece of wax paper between the window and the rim of the cup. Turn the cup over, holding the paper over the top of the cup so that the insect can't escape.
3. Now use the elastic band to hold the wax paper in place over the cup.

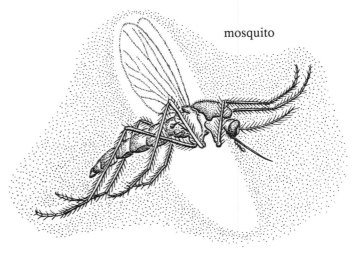

mosquito

4. Hold the cup to your ear and listen in. You will hear the insect buzzing very loudly. You may even be able to hear the insect's footsteps as it walks around. The sound has been *amplified* (made louder) by the cup and the paper. This is similar to the way a drum works when you beat it.
5. After listening to the insect, let it go.

The Cricket Weather Report

Want to know the temperature? The crickets will tell you.

What You Need:

a summer night when crickets
  are singing
a watch
pencil and paper
an outdoor thermometer, so that
  you can check your result

What To Do:

1. Cricket chirps are a familiar sound on late summer nights. Try to count the number of chirps you hear in 15 seconds. Use a watch so that you'll know when 15 seconds are up. Sometimes it's not easy to decide when one chirp ends and another begins. Give it a few tries.

2. First, let's find the temperature in Celsius. Take the number of cricket chirps you hear in 15 seconds. Divide this number by 2. Then add 6. The number you get is the temperature in Celsius. (Your answer should be within a couple of degrees of the actual temperature. Use a thermometer to check.) For example, suppose you heard 36 chirps in 15 seconds.

$$36 \div 2 = 18$$
$$18 + 6 = 24$$

   The temperature is about 24° C.

3. If you would like to find the temperature in Fahrenheit, do this. Take the number of cricket chirps you hear in 15 seconds. Add 40. The number you get is the temperature in Fahrenheit. For example, suppose you heard 36 chirps in 15 seconds.

$$36 + 40 = 76$$

   The temperature is about 76° F.

Fly By Nights

Here's an easy way to see some of the insects that only come out when the sun goes down.

What You Need:

a white sheet

a bright lamp (it could be a heavy duty flashlight or a desk lamp with an extension cord. You have to be able to *direct* its light.)*

What To do:

1. Hang up the white sheet outdoors. You might be able to hang it over a clothesline.
2. Wait until it is dark. Set up the light about a metre (a couple of feet) away from the sheet. Adjust it so that its light shines on the sheet.

3. After about an hour (and maybe sooner) you should find an interesting collection of insects on the sheet. They have been attracted by the light. You will probably have some moths, beetles and flies on your sheet. You may want to capture some of these insects, though, so that you can have a better look. Be sure to put each insect in a separate jar — or they might eat each other!
4. Try to find out what kinds of insects you have found. Don't keep them too long — let them go the next night.

*Insects are even more attracted by light that's invisible to us. It's called *ultraviolet*. "Dark lights" are special fluorescent lights that give off a lot of ultraviolet light. If you can get a dark light instead of an ordinary light, you will get many *more* insects.

Nature's Nightlights

Fireflies work their magic on summer nights in southern Canada and in the United States. They're not really flies, though; they're beetles. At night, the end section of their abdomens flash a bright greenish light. Fireflies can make this light with almost no heat. This is something the smartest human inventors can't do. (The light bulbs in your house become too hot to touch after they're left on for a short time.) Some female fireflies have no wings. They're called glowworms. Instead of flashing, they give off a steady glow. These lights let male and female fireflies find each other. Aren't we lucky that they make the nighttime more beautiful for people too!

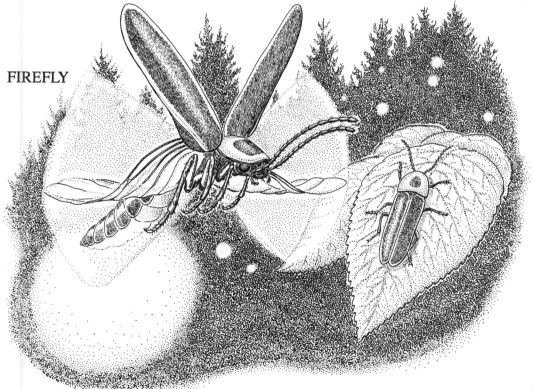

FIREFLY

What A Racket!

Have you ever passed workers who were breaking up the pavement with a pneumatic drill? Did you have to put your fingers in your ears because the noise was so loud? A large group of male cicadas clustered together can make as much noise as that drill! The cicada's loud hum is made when it vibrates drumlike organs on either side of its thorax. The sound of just one male cicada — the females make no sound at all — can be heard almost half a kilometre (more than a quarter of a mile) away. Is there anything in nature that can make these noisy insects shut up? Yes — a cicada killer — a wasp that hunts cicadas. If a cicada killer flies anywhere near a group of cicadas, they fall silent instantly.

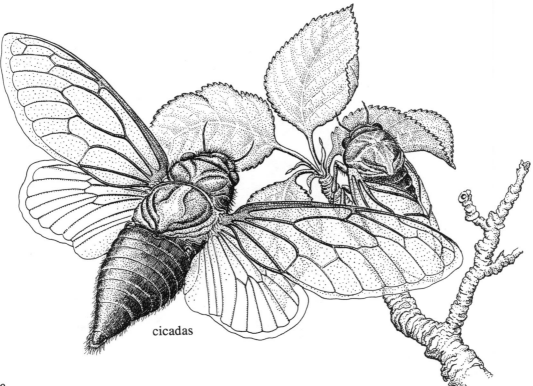

cicadas

Friends
Or Enemies?

You probably have a pretty good idea of who likes you and who doesn't. People are usually able to tell who their real friends are. But they're not so good at judging other kinds of animals. To some people, all insects are enemies: "Ugh! Nasty crawly things!" — Stamp! Swat! The fact is, most insects are harmless to human beings. They only want to go about their own lives. They don't deserve to be killed just because they happen to cross your path.

Have you ever thought about what the world would be like without insects? Many pleasing sights and sounds would disappear. There would be no brightly colored butterflies, and no crickets chirping on summer evenings. A lot of other things would be gone, too. Many birds, fish and other animals would die, because they need insects for food. Most flowering plants need insects to spread their pollen. Without insects, they would die out. Many of our fruits and vegetables come from these plants, so we'd be going hungry.

There'd be no honey for your toast without bees. There'd be no silk without caterpillars. On the other hand, things we *don't* want around would begin to pile up. Without scarab beetles to roll them away, the earth would be covered in animal droppings. Flies, carrion beetles and other insects feed or lay their eggs on decaying meat. Without them, dead bodies of animals would be lying everywhere.

There's no doubt that some insects have caused great suffering for human beings. Over the centuries, millions and millions of people have died of malaria. This is a disease spread by mosquitoes. Mosquitoes also spread many other serious diseases. The tsetse fly of Africa bites people and infects them with sleeping sickness. The bite of the rat flea spreads bubonic plague.

The ordinary housefly can be the worst disease spreader of all. Flies have hairy bodies and sticky foot pads. They pick up all sorts of germs when they walk through manure and decaying meat. Then they can bring these germs into people's houses. In some countries, people have no flush toilets, and no way to keep flies out of their houses or refrigerate their food. Flies in these places can spread a whole catalogue of terrible diseases. They include cholera, typhoid and diptheria.

Other insects can cause great damage to crops. Prairie farmers in the United States and Canada dread the huge swarms of grasshoppers that sometimes eat their grain. Almost every kind of plant people try to grow has an insect that eats it. Famines that have killed thousands of people have been caused by insects that destroyed the food supply.

People fight back against the insects, of course. They drain the swamps where mosquitoes breed. They find medicines to cure the sickness insects cause. Sometimes they spray the insects with poison chemicals. This works for a while. It is hard to wipe out insects this way, though. Insects usually have huge numbers of offspring. Suppose just a few are a little stronger than the others, so the poison cannot kill them. In a few weeks or months the survivors are laying eggs. This time, many of the new insects that hatch are strong, and poisons are unable to kill them.

In the meantime, the animals that eat insects may be poisoned by the chemicals. It's hard to spray insects with poison without hitting plants, so plants may be harmed. The poison also gets into the soil and into lakes and rivers. Since people eat plants and animals and drink water, the chemicals will finally get into their bodies too.

For these reasons, people keep looking for other ways to kill insect pests. We know that almost every insect has another insect that eats it. Sometimes the best way to get rid of a pest is to bring in a big supply of its worst enemy. About a hundred years ago, the orange trees of California were being killed by small insects called cottony-cushion scales. Lady bug beetles were brought over from Australia to eat them. Within a short time, the scales were controlled by the ladybugs, and the California orange crop was saved.

Do you understand better now why most insects should not be killed? They have their place in the world just as we do. Plants need them. The lives of many other creatures depend on them. And because they are food for so many animals, including other insects, most of them never become a problem for us.

Find An Aphid Colony

Aphids are tiny insects that live on plant juice. They're harmless for you to handle — they don't bite or sting. Yet many people think of them as enemies. This is because they produce babies so fast that they can overrun — and kill — your favorite garden plants.

What You Need:

a branch with aphids on it
scissors or a penknife

a glass jar about half full of water
a magnifying glass

What To Do:

1. Find a branch covered with aphids. Aphids are very small, round, pale green insects. They're easiest to find in the spring. You may see them on soft new plant shoots and flower buds. They especially love rose bushes.

2. ⊘ Cut off an aphid-covered branch. (Ask permission before you do this!) Bring it inside. Put it in the jar of water. (The water will keep the aphids on the branch.) Make sure that none of the aphids is underwater. Remove the branch and pour off some water if you need to.

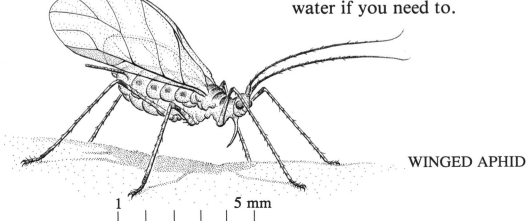

WINGED APHID

1   5 mm

3. Look at the aphids through the magnifying glass. Can you see their legs? How many do they have? Can you see their heads? Can you tell whether they are sucking juice from the branch? At the tips of their abdomens, you may see little drops of liquid. This is called honeydew, and ants love to drink it. Look for aphids that are larger than the others. You may see some of these large female aphids giving birth to babies. (Very few insects do this — most kinds lay eggs.)

4. Notice how much of the branch is covered with aphids. Leave the branch overnight and look at it again the next day. What do you see? Do you understand how such tiny insects can be very harmful to a garden?

MOTHER APHID GIVING BIRTH

Insect Wars

Here's the easiest way to get rid of some of the insects that harm your garden plants. Bring in other insects to eat them!

What You Need:

aphids on a branch
aphid-eating insects, such as
    earwigs, ladybugs or a
    praying mantis
a magnifying glass
newspaper
a small piece of paper

What to Do:

1. Collect some insects that are *predators* (insects that eat other insects). Earwigs and ladybugs eat aphids. (Page 11 tells you how to capture these insects without hurting them.) You'll likely find them near the plants that have aphids on them.

2. You may even find a praying mantis. If you do, don't be afraid of it. It *is* a large and fierce-looking insect. It has thick front legs with hooks on them. But its hooks won't hurt you. You may be able to capture it in your hands — but be careful not to squeeze it!

3. Lay the aphid branch on a piece of newspaper. Put your predators on a small piece of paper. Place the paper as close as you can to the aphids. Watch what happens through the magnifying glass.

How long does it take for a predator to find an aphid? How do the predators eat? (Some just bite — but a praying mantis will pick up the aphid between its front legs.)

Can you see how insects can be used to keep other insects from taking over the garden? Some garden supply stores sell ladybugs or mantis eggs to gardeners who don't want to use chemicals on their plants.

PRAYING MANTIS EATING APHIDS

The Deadly Fleas

In the fourteenth century, people all over Europe began to die of a mysterious disease. No one knew what was causing the sickness and there was no medicine for it. It was one of the biggest epidemics (outbreaks of sickness) that the world has ever known. And it was all caused by insects! In those days, almost everyone had rats in and around their houses. Some of these rats carried a disease called bubonic plague. The fleas that lived on these rats bit them. Then the fleas bit people and made them sick. Bubonic plague killed one-quarter of the people in Europe — about 25 million people!

Precious Cocoons

Soft, shimmering silk may be the most beautiful fabric in the world. You've probably heard that it comes from silkworms. But did you know that these "worms" are really caterpillars? Billions of these caterpillars are raised on farms in Japan. After a few weeks of eating mulberry leaves, the caterpillars lift their heads. A thin thread of silk comes out of their mouths. They wrap the threads round and round their bodies to make a cocoon. If they were left alone, they would hatch into moths. Instead, the cocoons are unwound on special machines. The fine silk strands are twisted together to form thicker threads. Then these threads are spun into silk cloth on other machines. It takes about 20,000 cocoons to make just 500 g (1 pound) of silk cloth.

SILKWORM

Insect Orders

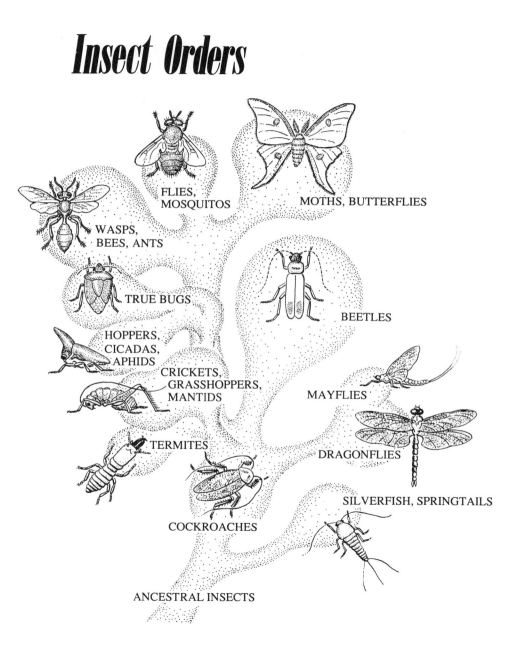

FLIES, MOSQUITOS

MOTHS, BUTTERFLIES

WASPS, BEES, ANTS

TRUE BUGS

BEETLES

HOPPERS, CICADAS, APHIDS

CRICKETS, GRASSHOPPERS, MANTIDS

MAYFLIES

TERMITES

DRAGONFLIES

SILVERFISH, SPRINGTAILS

COCKROACHES

ANCESTRAL INSECTS

Moths and Butterflies: Backyard Ballerinas

Moths and butterflies are the graceful ballet dancers of the insect world. Even people who think most insects are ugly or scary like to watch them. Their fluttering wings looks papery and delicate, but they are really quite strong. The skin of the wings is stretched over hard veins, just like a paper kite is stretched over a wooden frame. Moths and butterflies have two wings on each side. The front and back wings fit together so that they move like one big wing.

Moth and butterfly wings come in lots of different colors. Many of them are decorated with stripes and circles. These colors and designs are made by little overlapping scales that cover the wing. These scales are so tiny and soft that if you touch a wing they rub off like fine powder. If all the scales were taken off a moth's or butterfly's wing, it would look like clear, colorless cellophane!

Moths and butterflies have big eyes that take up most of their heads. They can see in all directions at once. They need to, because birds, frogs, toads, lizards and other animals like to eat them. They also have two long antennae which they use to smell and touch things.

Most butterflies and moths have long, hollow tongues. One kind of moth, the hawk moth, has a tongue that is 25 cm (10 inches) long. That's longer than a drinking straw, and six times as long as the moth's body! Why do they need such long tongues? Moths and butterflies live on nectar, the sweet juices of flowers. This juice is found deep inside the centers of flowers, where moths and butterflies can't go. Instead, they poke their tongues into the flowers and suck up the nectar. When they are not using their tongues, they keep them neatly rolled up.

Butterflies and moths begin their lives as tiny caterpillars. They hatch out of eggs. Most mammal babies — mammals are the family of animals *we* belong to — look like small versions of their mothers and fathers. But caterpillars look *nothing* like their parents. They have long, stretchy, bendable bodies. Some of them are smooth, some of them are covered with bumps, and some are furry or bristly.

Nearly all caterpillars are harmless to hold. It's fun to feel their sticky little feet tickle your arm. Woolly bears are especially cuddly-looking caterpillars, with bands of brown and black fur around their bodies. You can see them along country roads in most parts of North America. One caterpillar you should *not* pick up is the io. It's mostly green, with bands of reddish-brown and white along its sides. It's covered with bristles that can sting you.

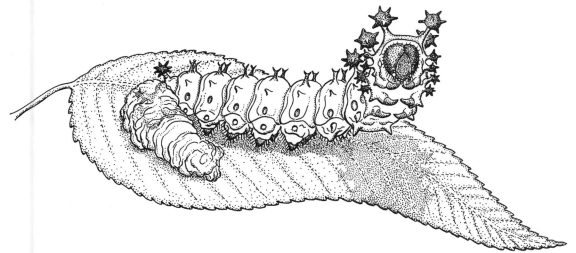

CECROPIA CATERPILLAR SPLITTING ITS SKIN

Caterpillars can only creep along very slowly. Fortunately, they don't have to go far. Usually they hatch right onto their own dinner plates — their favorite food plant. They begin to eat leaves. And eat and eat. As you would expect, they get bigger and fatter. When their skins get too tight, they split down the back. The caterpillar wiggles out of its old casing — and keeps on eating. Caterpillars may change their clothes five or six times before they're ready for their next adventure.

Often people say that butterflies hatch from *cocoons*. This isn't quite right. Moths are the insects that make cocoons — or rather their caterpillars do. Many moth caterpillars wrap themselves in these silk coats before they become pupae.

PAINTED LADY BUTTERFLY

Butterfly caterpillars do things a little differently. They attach themselves to a twig with a little blob of silk. Then they wriggle out of their caterpillar skin one last time. The coating underneath hardens to become a pupa case called a *chrysalis*. Inside cocoons and chrysalises, a magical change takes place. The creature that comes out of these casings, weeks or months later, is a crumpled-looking butterfly or moth. After its wings dry and straighten, it flies off to a new life.

You already know one difference between butterflies and moths — the way they spend their pupal stage. Do you know other ways to tell a butterfly from a moth? Well, if you see one of them going from flower to flower in the daytime, it's probably a butterfly. Butterflies like the sunlight. If you see one fluttering around your porchlight in the evenings, it's probably a moth. Most moths fly at night or very early in the morning.

Moths usually have thicker, furrier-looking bodies than butterflies. Their antennae are different, too. Butterfly antennae are long and thin, with a ball or hook on the end. Moth antennae are usually thicker and feathery looking. When they are at rest, moths hold their wings open, or flat against their bodies. Butterflies hold their wings together, standing straight up from their backs.

If you live in the eastern half of the continent, you may spot two of the largest moths in North America. The lovely luna moth is pale green with an "eye" spot on each wing. The cecropia moth is a dusty brown color and very big — about 13 cm (5 inches) across. There are many beautiful butterflies, too. Big orange, white and black monarchs can be found all over North America. Swallowtails, with their tiger stripes of yellow and black, are also common butterflies. All in all, there are about 10,000 kinds of butterflies and moths in North America. How many different ones can you spot?

Collect Some Cocoons

What You Need:
a penknife
a shoebox
a notebook
a pencil

What To Do:

1. Look outdoors for moth cocoons. You can find them year round. You might see them on leaves, branches, tree bark, shrubs, fence posts, window sills, or inside garages or sheds. Sometimes you may find them on the ground, among dead leaves or under stones. If you search patiently, you'll be sure to discover some cocoons.

2. You have to handle a cocoon carefully, so that the pupa inside won't be hurt. Be very gentle when you take the cocoon from the place where you find it. Put it in a shoebox to carry it home.

3. ⊘You may find a cocoon attached to a small branch of

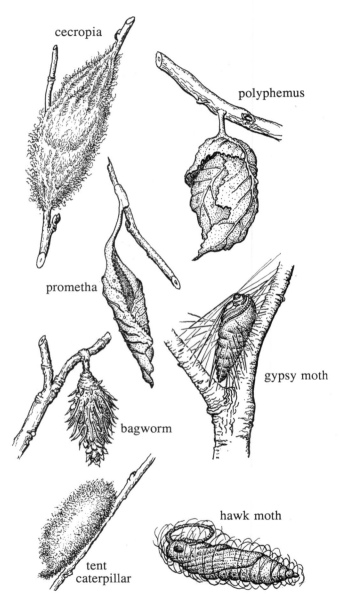

cecropia

polyphemus

prometha

bagworm

gypsy moth

tent caterpillar

hawk moth

a tree or shrub. Don't try to pull off the cocoon. It is best to use a penknife to cut the twig that holds the cocoon.

4. Write in your notebook where you found the cocoon, and when you found it. Later, if you find out what kind of cocoon it is, you can add the name of the moth that made it. (Use library reference books to find out about the cocoons you collect.)

5. You may find a cocoon that has no pupa in it. Or the pupa may have died. Here are some ways to tell:

(a) Empty cocoons or cocoons with dead pupae inside are lighter than cocoons with live pupae inside. After you've collected a few cocoons, you'll be able to feel the difference in weight.

(b) Some cocoons are thin. You can see whether there is a pupa inside.

(c) Shake the cocoon *very gently,* near your ear. If there is a live pupa inside, you will hear it bump against the case. If you hear a rattle, the cocoon is probably empty. The rattle is caused by the dry skin the moth left behind when it came out of the cocoon.

(d) You may see an opening in an empty cocoon that the moth made when it left. A large jagged hole in the cocoon might mean that a bird, mouse or squirrel ate the pupa.

(e) If there are many tiny holes in the cocoon, the pupa inside will probably not turn into a moth. The ichneumon wasp makes holes in a cocoon and lays her eggs inside. When the ichneumon larvae hatch, they feed on the pupa.

6. All cocoons are interesting to collect and look at. But if you find one with a live pupa, you can keep it until the moth comes out. You will learn how on page 56.

Moth Magic

Think of this as a magic show for patient people. It may take months for the moth to come out of the cocoon, but it's an exciting day when it does.

What You Need:

a 1 L (1 quart) glass jar
   with a wide mouth
a small branch
a piece of fine wire screen
a thick elastic band
a cocoon with a pupa inside

1. Place the cocoon carefully in the jar. (A wide-mouthed jar makes this easier to do. And later, the moth can leave the jar without getting hurt.)
2. Put a small branch inside the jar. This will give the moth something to cling to.
3. Put a piece of fine wire screen over the top of the jar. Hold it in place with a thick elastic band. Now the cocoon can get air, but it is protected from mice and squirrels. Later, the screen will keep the moth from escaping.
4. It is best to keep the jar outside, *in a sheltered spot*. An unheated porch or balcony would be ideal. You can also put the jar between a window and a window screen, or on a sheltered window ledge. This way, the cocoon is outside but you can watch it from inside. The cocoon can stay outside even in winter. After all, if you hadn't found it, the cocoon would have wintered outdoors.
5. When will your moth come out? Probably in the spring or summer. You may get some warnings that the moth is about to appear. The pupa may begin to wiggle enough to shake the cocoon. Maybe you will hear scratching sounds from inside the

cocoon. The end of the cocoon where the moth will come out may get wet. However, a lot of cocoons give no warning at all. Your best bet is to check the cocoon every day, especially in the morning. (Many kinds of moths come out of their cocoons in the morning.)

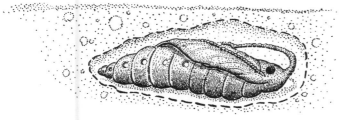

HAWK MOTH COCOON

A NEWLY EMERGED HAWK MOTH DRYING ITS WINGS

6. The exciting day finally arrives. If you're lucky, you'll be there to see the moth come out. You may be surprised by how it looks. When the moth first appears, it is wet and crumpled. Over the next few hours, though, its wings fill out and its body dries. Finally the moth is ready to fly. Wish it a safe journey and open the jar so that it can take off on its new wings.

How Much Lunch Can a Caterpillar Munch?

Just how much can a hungry caterpillar eat in one day? You can find out with some graph paper.

What You Need:

a caterpillar
a jar with a screen lid, like the
    one on page 81.
a plant for the caterpillar to eat
2 pieces of graph paper

What To Do:

1. Find a caterpillar and put it in a jar. You need the right kind of food for your caterpillar. Many of them eat only one kind of plant. Very likely the plant on which you find the caterpillar is the food it likes. Bring home a branch of this plant.

2. Use a piece of graph paper with small squares. Lay the plant on the paper. Carefully, without hurting the plant, trace *all* its leaves onto the paper. Your graph paper should now look like the drawing.

3. Put the plant branch in the jar with the caterpillar. Put the jar in a quiet place out of direct sunlight. Leave the caterpillar alone for one day so that it can eat as much as it wants.

4. Count the squares on your graph paper that are covered by plant leaves. If a square is less than half covered, don't

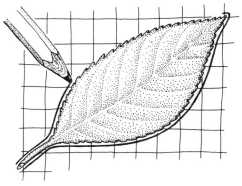

count it. If it is more than half covered, count it as a whole square.

5. After a day, take the plant out of the caterpillar jar. The leaves probably have lots of holes in them. Lay *all* the leaves on the second piece of graph paper. (Its squares have to be the same size as the ones on the first piece you used.) Trace around them. If there are holes in the middle of the leaves, trace around the holes too.

6. How many squares do the leaves cover now? Subtract the number of squares the munched leaves cover from the number that the fresh

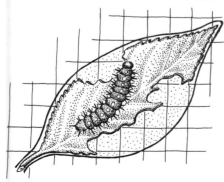

leaves cover. The difference is the amount the caterpillar ate.

Let's try an example. Suppose that we used paper divided into one millimeter squares. We count up the leaf covered squares and this is what we get:

area of the fresh leaves   162 mm²
area of the chewed leaves 111 mm²

How many square millimeters of leaf did the caterpillar eat in one day?

162 mm² − 111 mm² = 51 mm²
Try it with your caterpillar and see if it eats this much.

7. Think about how much salad you might eat for lunch. Think about how big you are. Think about how small the caterpillar is, and how much "salad" it ate. Are you impressed by its appetite?

8. Put the caterpillar back where you found it.

The Amazing Eating Machine

The larva of the polyphemus moth eats 86,000 times its birthweight in the first 48 hours of its life. It grows to be a large fat green caterpillar almost 8 cm (over 3 inches) long.

Monarch Migrations

When you watch butterflies flutter from flower to flower, they don't look strong enough to go very far. But some butterflies migrate like birds. Every September, monarch butterflies fly from Canada to spend the winter in Florida, Mexico and California. Some of them go 3,000 km (over 1,850 miles) to escape the cold. In March, the children of these butterflies — who hatched in the south and have never seen Canada — somehow find their way north again!

Super Flutter

When the Queen Alexandra birdwing butterfly flutters by, people in New Guinea sit up and take notice. It's the world's largest known butterfly, with a wingspan of 21 cm (over 8 inches). That's about as big as a large magazine page. And there's a moth in New Guinea that's even bigger — the hercules moth has a wingspread of 28 cm (over 11 inches). These two giants are about *three times* the size of a monarch butterfly.

Beetles Are Everywhere!

Lady bug, lady bug, fly away home
Your house is on fire
And your children are in bed

We all know the words to say when we catch a ladybug. The ladybug is one of our best friends. Its larvae eat other insects like aphids that cause a lot of damage to our garden plants.

The lady*bug* is not really a bug at all. It belongs to a group of insects called *beetles*. Look under a log or rock even in winter and you are likely to find beetles. They can be found in puddles, cold mountain streams, in deserts and on mountaintops.

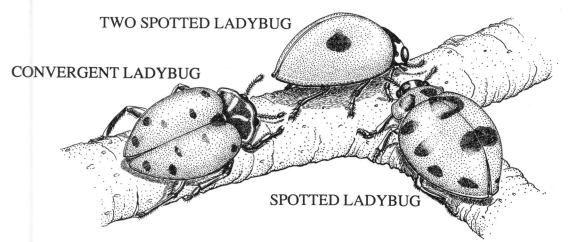

TWO SPOTTED LADYBUG

CONVERGENT LADYBUG

SPOTTED LADYBUG

Of all the kinds of insects, about one-third or about 330,000, are beetles. There are as many beetles as there are different kinds of plants in the world! They come in many sizes, shapes and colors. They happen to be my favorite group of insects.

Just what are beetles? They all have a hard outer pair of wings called the *elytra*. These serve as protective covers for the fragile, membrane-like wings they actually use for flying. Beetles vary in size from microscopic to some of the largest of all insects. One of the most striking features of beetles is their antennae, which they use for tasting, smelling and touching. Look closely at the heads of different beetles and you will be amazed at the variety of antennae.

Many beetles cause a great deal of damage. They burrow in trees and ruin the wood. They suck the juices out of crops such as cotton. But they also control other insect pests by eating them. They clean up a lot of the garbage that occurs in nature, too. Let's meet a few.

Whirligig beetles are those crazy looking things twirling so fast on the surface of ponds that you can't see what they look like. Although they move on the water's surface, they aren't waterproof underneath. Their sides are flattened to rest on the water and keep them afloat. If you put detergent in the water to reduce the surface tension, whirligigs can't stay up, and they sink. When they dive for food, they carry a bubble of air down with them.

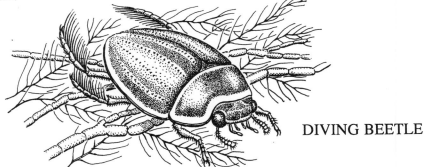

DIVING BEETLE

Out in a forest you may come across a dead mouse or snake. If you go back to look for it the next day it may be gone. Did another animal eat it? Often the carcass is still nearby, but buried — by carrion beetles! These are nature's garbage collectors. A male and female will work as a pair. If they can't dig the ground around the body, they move it by lying on their backs and pushing it along with their feet. They dig holes and bury the body. Then the female lays eggs in it so that their larvae will have something to feed on. In this way, carrion beetles clean up the forests for us.

The ancient Egyptians worshipped all kinds of creatures, but one of the most unusual was the scarab or dung beetle. Many of their ornaments showed carvings of the beetle. Like the carrion beetles, scarabs get rid of waste. Some kinds of dung beetles make a ball of animal droppings (dung). Then they roll it to a selected spot where they dig a hole and put the ball into it. Next, they lay eggs in the ball and cover it up. If it weren't for these insects, fields could be covered with a thick, hard layer of dried dung.

One of the most spectacular beetles is found in wooded areas. This is the stag beetle or pinching bug, which can read 60 mm (over 2 inches) in length. The male has a huge set of jaws that it uses for defense. If it is threatened, it raises its head high and holds these jaws wide open. That's enough to scare off a lot of its enemies!

Click beetles have a head and thorax that can be moved up and down from the abdomen. If you catch one and put it on its back, you'll see it tilt its head back and give a quick snap up. Flip! The beetle will pop right side up. It's a remarkable way to make sure that it doesn't end up like a turtle on its back, unable to turn itself over.

We've barely started to tell you about all the beetles there are in the world. You have an idea, though, why they are such favorites to many insect lovers.

A Trap for Beetles

It's not easy to catch ground beetles, because they run along the ground very quickly. This is a way to trap them so that you can have a closer look.

What You Need:

a tin can with the lid removed
a garden trowel

BEETLE TRAP

What to Do:

1. Find a patch of earth in a garden. Ask permission before you dig. Use the trowel to dig a hole for your tin can.
2. Set the can in the earth so that its rim is level with the ground. Pack in the soil around the can so that there are no spaces.
3. Check your trap night and morning. Have you caught any beetles? Do you think that these beetles hunt at night or in the daytime?
4. Try putting in beetle traps in different places — under trees, in a weed patch, near a lawn. (Again — get permission *before* you dig.) Where do you have the best luck catching beetles?
5. After you've had a good look at your beetles (and maybe tried the activity on page 65), let them go.

Beetle Footprints

You've probably seen lots of human footprints, and dog and cat pawprints, too. But have you ever seen an insect's footprints? Now you can.

What You Need:

a beetle
some food coloring (you can get
    this at the grocery store)
a small plate
a sheet of paper

BEETLE FOOTPRINTS

What to Do:

1. Catch a beetle (see page 64). Put it in the refrigerator — in a jar, of course — for about 10 minutes. This will slow it down and make it easier for you to handle.
2. Put a couple of drops of food coloring on a plate. Don't make a pool that would be deep for the beetle. You want it to walk through the food coloring so that just its feet and the tip of its abdomen get wet.
3. Have the beetle walk through the food coloring and then walk across the sheet of paper. What kind of a trail does it leave? You will probably find a zigzag pattern across your paper. Do you think the beetle runs on the tips of its feet, or does it leave a longer mark on the paper?
4. You might like to try this with some other kinds of insects. Do they all make zigzags?

Beetle Giants

The biggest insects in the world are the goliath beetles of Equatorial Africa. These heavyweight champs have a mass of 100 g (3 ½ ounces) and can be up to 11 cm (4½ inches) long. They are fierce looking insects with thick, shiny "armor." They're harmless to people, though. African children sometimes attach strings to these beetles and fly them in circles like model airplanes! Nearly as big and even fiercer looking are the elephant beetles of Central America and the West Indies. These beetles have big jutting horns that take up one-quarter of their length.

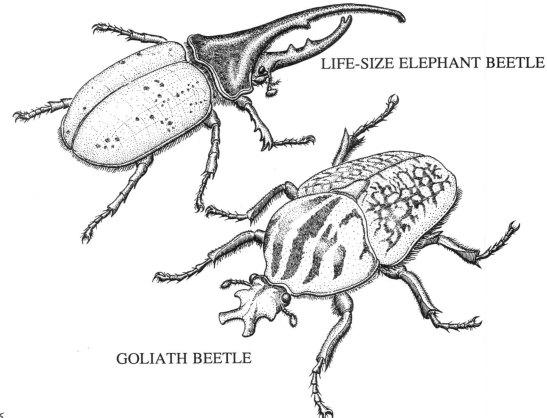

LIFE-SIZE ELEPHANT BEETLE

GOLIATH BEETLE

Bees: Flowers' Best Friends

*T*he next time you are walking in a flower garden, enjoying the colors and scents of the flowers, think about this. The flowers aren't putting on this display for you or any other person. The bright colors and the perfume are the flowers' way of advertising to bees: we've got food for you!

Bees couldn't live without flowers. And many flowers couldn't live without bees. All of the bees' food comes from flowers. They suck nectar — the sweet juice of the flower — with their long tongues. They also collect pollen for food. This is a fine yellow powder that the flower makes.

To make seeds that will grow into new plants, pollen has to be spread from flower to flower. Plants can't move. Instead, they get bees to do the work of *pollination* for them.

Bees don't care about pollinating flowers. It's just something that happens while they're gathering food. Sticky pollen gets caught in the hairs on the bees' body. Some of it is eaten by the bees. Some of it is swept into "shopping bags" on the bees' hind legs. This food is carried back to the nest. But some of the pollen is dusted off as the bees travel from one flower to another. And this is how the flowers are pollinated.

If you were asked to draw a bee, what would you put in your picture? Most people would give it black and yellow stripes. And they'd show its body ending in the sharp point of its stinger. This would make a good drawing of a honeybee or (if you made your bee fat and fuzzy) a bumble-bee. But there are many kinds of bees in the world. There are black bees, blue bees — even red bees. Some of these bees have no stingers. Even among bumblebees and honeybees, only the females can sting.

In North America, only bumblebees and honeybees live in big groups. They're called *social bees*. Most kinds of bees live on their own. They're called *solitary bees*. Their homes are usually burrows in the ground. The social bees live together in nests. Bumblebees usually make their nests in the ground, in empty burrows left by chipmunks or mice. Wild honeybees usually make their nests in hollow trees. Most honey-bees live in *hives*, special houses built for them by people.

People raise honeybees so that they can collect their honey. Honey is a food made by bees from nectar and their own body juices. Because honeybees are important to us, we've learned quite a bit about how they live. The honeybee nest is made up of many small cells built of *beeswax*. Each cell has six sides and they all fit neatly together to form a *honey-comb*. But only some of these cells are filled with honey. Others contain stored pollen. And still others are nurseries for eggs and larvae.

Like ants, honeybees have a large queen who lays eggs, thousands of female workers, and a few males. The younger workers keep busy inside the nest. They build and repair cells, feed the larvae and look after the queen. If it gets too cold in the hive, workers will huddle over the larvae to make a living blanket. If it gets too hot, workers stand at the entrance of the hive and fan their wings to cool it down!

Some older workers are guards for the hive. They will sting their enemies to kill them or drive them away. Each honeybee can only sting once, though. Its stinger stays inside its victim. Without its stinger, the honeybee dies.

Other older workers fly off to look for food. If they find some, they come back to the hive and tell the others. Then a large group of bees go out together to share in the food-gathering work.

If you had something very important to tell a friend, what would you do? You might telephone. If your friend lives close by, you might run over to tell him or her. If you were *very* excited about your news, you might be hopping up and down or dancing around. Your friend would know you were excited, but not why, until you were calm enough to speak.

Honeybees have exciting news for each other, too. One worker has to spread the news about the wonderful patch of flowers she has found. But she has no voice to speak. So what does she do? She "dances" a message for the other bees! If the food is close by, she does a round dance. If it's far away, she dances a pattern that looks like a fat figure eight. By how quickly she does her dance, and how many waggles she puts into it, the other bees can figure out just how far away the food is.

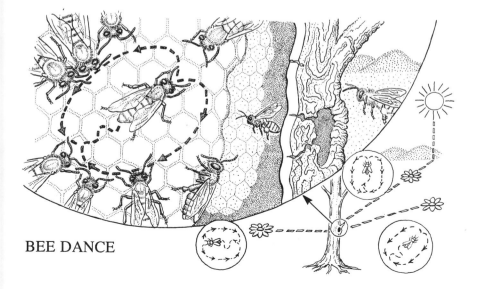

BEE DANCE

And here's something even more amazing. The other bees can also learn which direction they should go. The bee who found the food somehow judges the angle made by the food, the hive and the sun (see the drawings). She will put the same angle into her dance! Then off the honeybees will go to the flowers, to gather their food and — quite by chance — make it possible for us to have a beautiful garden.

Wide-Bodied Jumbos

Even when a bumble bee is not carrying anything, it seems surprising that its little papery wings could lift that big fuzzy body. But when the bumble bee flies home to its nest, it's really loaded down. In fact, it may be carrying *more than its own weight* in nectar and pollen. A jumbo jet can only carry about 40 percent of its weight in cargo and people.

WIDE-BODIED BUMBLE BEE

Watch Some Bee-havior

Because it's not safe for us to peer inside a beehive, we don't usually see bees making honey or doing their dances. Here are some ideas for getting honeybees to do interesting things while you can watch them.

What You Need:

a plate with a few drops of water
    mixed with sugar
a plate with a few drops of water
    mixed with artificial sweetener
two jars
two small pieces of wire window
    screen

What to Do:

1. Find a patch of flowers that honeybees like to visit. From a safe distance, watch them going about their work. Can you see the bright yellow pollen bags on their hind legs?

2. Watch a honeybee move from flower to flower. Is there a pattern to the way it goes? Does it ever visit a flower twice? (Here are some patterns people have noticed. On Queen Anne's Lace, which has many small flowers

pollen bags

joined together, the bee starts at the edge of the flower cluster and works towards the center. On spike-shaped flowers such as loosestrife, the bee usually starts at the bottom and works up.)

3. Put the plate with a few drops of sugar water on it near the flower patch. Then move away and watch what happens. Soon a honeybee will find the plate. What does it do?

4. After a while, the honeybee will probably go back to its nest. Keep track of how long it takes for a group of bees to come to your plate. What do you think happened when the first bee went back to the hive?

5. The next day, put out two plates. On one, put sugar water. On the other, put water mixed with artificial sweetener (this has no food value for the bees). Do the honeybees go to both plates? Do they seem to like one plate better than the other?

6. Bees need water in hot weather. (You can sometimes see them drinking at a puddle.) They are very good at finding water, even without touching it. You can prove this for yourself. Instead of the sugar plates, put out two jars. Fill one half full of water. Put a piece of wire screen over the top. Put a piece of screen over the empty bottle, too. The bottles look the same, but the honeybees know they're different. Which bottle do they go to?

Make Some Clover Syrup

No creature but a honeybee can take some flower nectar and turn it into honey. But you can make a sweet, nectary syrup out of clover, one of the bee's favorite flowers.

What You Need:

1 kg (2 lbs.) sugar
350 mL (1⅓ cups) water
1 mL (¼ tsp.) alum (you can get this at the drugstore)
a large saucepan
a piece of cheesecloth
a large, heatproof bowl
a wide-mouthed jar or bottle, with a lid
40 white clover heads, 20 red clover heads, and 3 rose petals

What to Do:

1. ⊘ Pick the flower heads you need. Ask an adult to help you find a field or garden that has *not* been sprayed with chemicals.
2. Wash the flower heads and put them in a heatproof bowl.
3. ⊘ Put the sugar, the water, and the alum in a saucepan. Bring to a boil for 5 minutes.
4. ⊘ Pour the liquid over the flowers. Let the bowl of syrup cool for 20 minutes.
5. Strain the syrup through a piece of cheesecloth and put it in a bottle or jar. You will have about 750 mL (3 cups) of sweet syrup with the faint taste of clover. Try it on some pancakes!

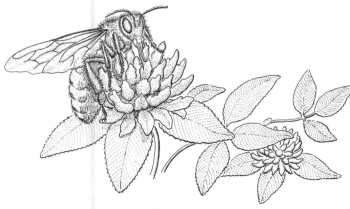

HONEYBEE SUCKING NECTAR

Have a Honey Treat

Bees had to make about 80,000 trips to flowers to gather one jar of honey for you. You'll be thankful for all that hard work when you taste these yummy treats.

What You Need:

250 mL (1 cup) peanut butter
250 mL (1 cup) honey — use a
    little less if honey is very
    liquid
250 mL (1 cup) milk powder
Chopped dried apricots, dates,
    apples or walnuts
Sesame seeds or toasted coconut
medium mixing bowl
large spoon
wax paper
cookie sheet

What to Do:

1. Spread a piece of wax paper on a cookie sheet.
2. In a mixing bowl, mix together the peanut butter, honey and milk powder. Stir in the chopped fruit or nuts.
3. Using your hands, form the mixture into balls about 3-5 cm (1-2 in.) in diameter. Roll the balls in sesame seeds or coconut.
4. Put the balls on the wax papered cookie sheet. Chill them in the refrigerator for an hour. This recipe makes about 18 peanut butter-honey balls.

Ants:
The Non-Stop
Workers

Ants live in a family, just as you do. But in some ant families, everybody has thousands of relatives. They all live together in an ant nest. Their nest is usually an underground "city" with many rooms and winding tunnels. And all these ants have the same mother!

This mother is called the "queen." She is much larger than the other ants. She does nothing but lay eggs. Other female ants — called worker ants — feed the queen and take care of her eggs.

Soft white larvae hatch out of these eggs. The workers feed the larvae. They also carry the larvae outside in good weather. This is rather like taking a baby out for a walk in a stroller!

Soon the larvae roll themselves up into cocoons. When the new adults are ready to hatch, the workers cut open the cocoon with their jaws. The new ants are pale and weak. After a while, their shells harden and become darker. They're ready to go to work.

Maybe you help your family by making your bed or taking out the garbage. But you also have time to play and relax. Worker ants keep very busy. They may be cleaning out the nest. They carry dead ants, old cocoons and food leftovers to their garbage dump. Other workers are building new tunnels and rooms, with no tools but their jaws. They use their saliva as cement.

Older workers go out of the nest to look for food. Some kinds of ants don't see very well. However, they can smell with their antennae. They follow an odor trail laid down by other ants from their nest. When two ants meet on the trail, they tap each other with their antennae. They can tell whether the other ant is a sister or a stranger by its smell. Some kinds of ants are meat eaters. They kill insects, worms and snails much bigger

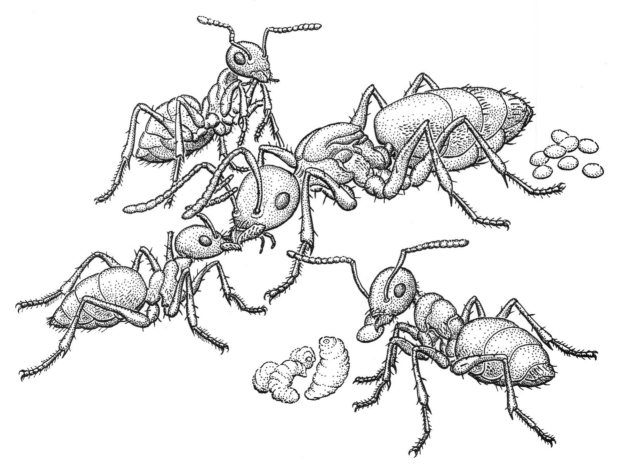

QUEEN ANT WITH WORKERS, EGGS AND LARVAE

than they are by attacking in groups. Then the ants work together to cut up the food and carry or drag it back to the nest.

Other kinds of ants eat seeds and plant juices. Some kinds even become farmers. Human farmers keep herds of cows for their milk. Ant farmers take care of small insects called aphids. Aphids suck the juice from plant stems. Ants know that if they stroke the aphids with their antennae, the aphids will produce a drop of honeydew. This is a sweet liquid that ants love. The ants carry their aphids from plant to plant. They also protect the aphids from ladybugs who want to eat them.

The biggest, strongest workers become guards and soldiers. They tap each new arrival at the nest with their antennae. Only the ants that belong to the nest have the right smell. Everybody else is driven away. They will defend the nest fiercely, using their strong jaws to bite. Some ants can burn and blind their enemies by squirting acid from the ends of their bodies.

A few of the ants born in the nest don't have to work. These special ants have wings. Some of them are males and some are females. The workers look after them until they are ready to leave the nest.

Then, one special day, swarms of winged ants rise in the air. The males and females mate while flying. Soon after, the males sink to the ground and die. The females, though, are about to begin the greatest adventure of their lives. Many will be eaten by birds and spiders. But a few — the quickest and the luckiest — will become queens.

Each queen pulls off her wings as quickly as she can. She doesn't need them any more and they slow her down. Then she looks for a cool, dark place where she can start her nest. She may go under a stone or into a crack in the earth. There she lays her first eggs and waits for them to hatch. After a few months, a new ant family will be working busily in its new home.

Let's Go Ant Watching

What You Need:

a plastic bag with a little sugar in it

a plastic bag with a little grass seed in it

a plastic bag with a few bacon bits in it

a magnifying glass

What to Do:

1. Look around outside for some scurrying ants. You might find them in your backyard or on a sidewalk.
2. Scatter a few grains of sugar in the ants' path. What do the ants do?
3. See if you can find an ant's nest. It usually looks like a mound of sand, with an opening in the top. Scatter a few grains of sugar at the opening of the ant's nest. What happens?
4. Now try scattering a little grass seed, or a few bits of bacon. What happens? Are you learning what ants like to eat?
5. Watch the ants through your magnifying glass as they leave and come back to the nest. Are any of them carrying anything into the nest? What? Are they carrying anything out? How do they carry things? What happens if another insect goes near the opening of the nest?
6. Follow some ants as they go about their work. Do they seem to have a regular route that they take? When two ants meet, what do they do? Do they ever bump into each other? What happens when an ant meets another insect?
7. Now that you know so much about ants, you might like to write a story about an ant's adventures, or draw a picture showing ants at work.

Start an Ant Village

Do the project on page 78 first, to get to know something about ant life. Then start an "ant village" in a jar.

What You Need:

plastic bags with twist ties
newspaper
a shovel
a small bucket
a large spoon
a large glass jar (the kind used
    for preserving) with a metal
    screw top and sealer
pieces of fine window screen
a block of wood
a small piece of plastic sponge,
    about 2 cm × 2 cm (1 in.
    square)
black construction paper
for food: grass seed, sugar

What to Do:

1. ⊘ Remove the sealer top from the jar. Separate the sealer lid from the metal ring. Using the sealer lid as a size guide, cut two circles of window screen. (Ask a grownup to do this for you.) Two circles are needed to help prevent the ants from escaping.

2. Put a block of wood in the middle of the jar. This will keep the ants near the sides of the jar, where you can see them at work.

3. Find an ant's nest. Spread the newspaper beside it. Dig down with the spade into the earth. Put the loose soil on the piece of newspaper. Look for ants, ant cocoons (they look like grains of rice), and larvae. Try hard to find a queen ant, because your ant village can't live long without her. She is much larger than any of the other ants. Use the spoon to place all these creatures in the plastic bags.

Work carefully so that ants and larvae are not harmed. Try to get about 30 to 50 ants who belong to the nest. It's important not to add any ants who are outsiders — the other ants will kill them.

4. Put enough earth in the bucket to fill your glass jar ¾ full. Return home.

5. Put the plastic bags with the ants inside in the refrigerator for about 10 minutes. Don't forget about them! The cold will slow down the ants so that you can move them more easily. Put the ants in the jar. Again, work carefully so that they are not harmed.

6. Put the two circles of screen over the jar right away, before your ants can escape. Screw the metal ring down tight to hold the screen in place.

7. Give your ants some food. Remove the ring and lift an edge of the screen, being careful not to let your ants escape. Put a small piece of plastic sponge, wetted with water, on top of the soil. If you keep the sponge moist, this will give your ants all the

DETAIL OF ANT NEST

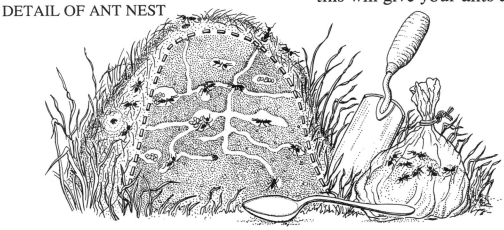

water they need. Scatter some grass seed or a few grains of sugar on the earth. The ants may also like bread or cake crumbs or tiny bits of fruit and vegetable. You will soon get to know what they like.

8. Screw the metal jar ring on, to hold the two circles of screen in place. Wrap the sides of the jar with black construction paper. Tape it in place. Leave the paper loose so that you can lift it off to look at the ants. Lift the paper only when you want to see what the ants are doing.

9. Keep your ants at room temperature. Don't put the jar in direct sunlight, and don't put it near a radiator.

10. Every other day, remove any uneaten food and give the ants fresh food.

11. The ants will take a little while to feel at home in the jar. Once they do, they will begin to build rooms and tunnels in the earth. You will see how they collect food from the top of the earth and store it. You will also see the bits of earth that they carry to the top as they dig their tunnels.

12. After you have watched your ant village for a couple of weeks, let the ants go free at the place where you caught them.

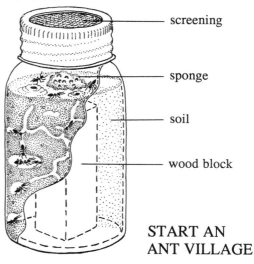

screening

sponge

soil

wood block

START AN
ANT VILLAGE

Underground Farmers

People in tropical parts of South America sometimes come upon a strange sight. They see two long lines of marching ants. The two lines are going in opposite directions. And in one line, the ants seem to be carrying little green parasols! These are leaf cutter ants. They travel more than a kilometre (up to a mile) to get to their favorite leaves. Every ant cuts a neat little triangle out of a leaf. Then they make the journey back to their underground nest. Each ant carries its leaf on its back. After all this work, you'd expect the ants to rest and eat their leaves. But they don't. They carry the leaves down into big underground rooms they have made. They chew the leaves into little pieces and spread them around. And then they wait. After a while, fungus begins to grow on the leaves. And then these tiny farmers finally dine — on the fungus!

Terrifying Warriors

In Africa and South America, there are creatures so fierce that every animal flees from them. People in villages leave their homes to escape them. Even elephants run away. What are these mighty warriors? They're ants! Millions of army ants go on the march together. Their column can be almost a metre (3 feet) across, and hundreds of metres long. Even rivers don't stop these ants. Some of the ants link their legs to form a living bridge across the water. Then the other ants swarm across.

As the army moves through the countryside, the ants eat every living thing in their path — other insects, snakes and birds. They can also eat large animals if the animals are fenced in or for some other reason can't run away. Is there anything good to say about army ants? Well, yes. After the army has passed by, the villagers return home. They find that their homes have been swept clean of pests like rats and fleas.

Living Lunchboxes

What's round and yellow, hangs from the ceiling, and gives out lunch whenever it's asked? Give up? It's an ant. Every ant has two stomachs. It has its own private stomach to digest its food, just as you do. But it also has a stomach for sharing, called a *crop*. A worker comes back to the nest bringing food in its crop. Another ant will come up and ask for food. It does this by stroking the first ant with its antennae. The ant that gathered the food will bring up some of it and give it to the hungry ant.

Honey pot ants go even farther than this in sharing food. These ants gather sweet plant juice. Then they overfeed some of their sisters. These overfed ants become so big and round that they can't walk. They just hang from the roof of the nest all day, looking like fat yellow jewels. If the honeypot ants run short of food, they just ask their living lunchboxes for a meal!

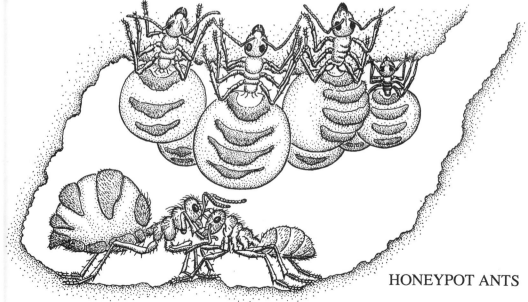

HONEYPOT ANTS

Spiders: Insects' Relatives

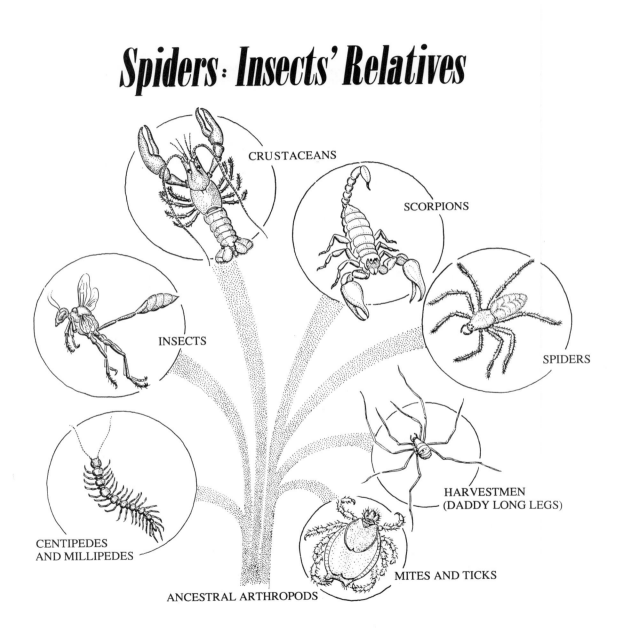

CRUSTACEANS

SCORPIONS

INSECTS

SPIDERS

CENTIPEDES
AND MILLIPEDES

HARVESTMEN
(DADDY LONG LEGS)

MITES AND TICKS

ANCESTRAL ARTHROPODS

Spiders: Web-Spinning Wizards

Would you like to have some extra eyes? A couple of eyes in the back of your head might be handy. No one would ever be able to sneak up on you. And one on each side of your head would make it safer to cross the street. Most spiders have eight eyes — and they can see in all directions at once!

Spiders are distant cousins of insects. Like insects, they wear their skeletons on the outside. But they have only two body parts. Their heads and thoraxes are joined together in one part called a *cephalothorax*. They also have an *abdomen*. And here's the difference that's easiest to spot between insects and spiders — all spiders have eight legs. (As you already know, insects get along fine with six.) Spiders belong to a class of animals called *arachnida*. Some of the spiders' relatives are ticks, mites, and scorpions.

Like insects, spiders lay eggs. But they don't go through a larval stage. Little spiders hatch out of the eggs looking just like their parents, except that they're much smaller. As they grow bigger, they shed their skins many times. If all the little spiders stayed in the place where they hatched, they would have to fight each other for food. In fact, they might even eat each other. They need to travel far away for food. How do you think they do it?

Spiders don't have wings. But they do have a way to fly through the air when they need to. They produce fine strong strands of silk from six *spinnerets* on their abdomens. The silk is liquid, but it dries as soon as the air touches it. When the spiders want to travel, they raise their abdomens and send out a strand of silk. The silk thread is caught by the breeze. The spider is carried off through the air. This is called ballooning. Although most of them only go up a few hundred metres, ballooning spiders have been found 4200 m (14,000 feet) up in the air! Spiders also use shorter silk strands as bridges from one place to another.

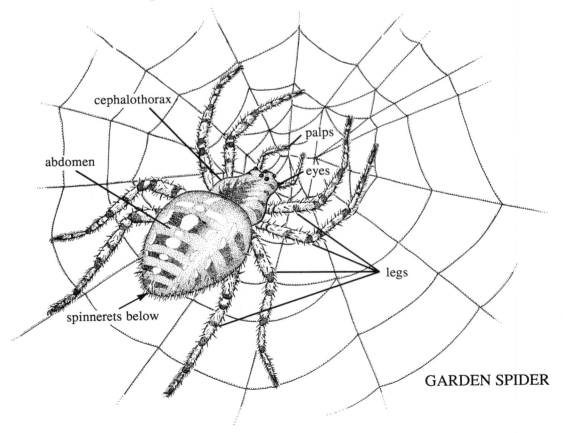

cephalothorax

palps

eyes

abdomen

legs

spinnerets below

GARDEN SPIDER

All spiders are hunters. They use their fangs to poison their prey. Then they suck out its body juices, leaving a little dried husk. When we think of spiders, we think of webs in which the spider sits waiting for a fly to be caught. But, while all spiders can make silk, not all spiders spin webs to catch food.

Wolf spiders suddenly jump on their prey. The biggest spiders — the tarantulas — build burrows in the ground. These burrows have hinged trap-doors on them. The tarantulas hide there until they can ambush a passing grasshopper, beetle or other unlucky insect. The bola spider captures moths by hurling a silk thread with a sticky glob on the end of it.

Some spiders spin messy looking webs. The cobwebs that you sometimes see in the corners of rooms are just loose masses of spider silk spun by house spiders.

The most beautiful spider webs are called *orb webs*. Spiders who live in gardens and backyards make these lacy wonders. First the spider spins several strong lines from which the web will hang. Next the spider lays down the long lines from the centre of the web out to the edge. They look like the spokes of a wheel. Last comes the sticky part in which insects will be caught — the spiral that connects all the spokes. The spider has oil on its feet so that it does not stick to its own web.

When the web is finished, the spider hides and waits. The struggles of a trapped insect make the web tremble. The spider runs to its prey and wraps it round and round in silk. This tidy little package will be ready whenever the spider feels like a meal.

The spider spins its web to catch food, not to impress people. But when you see a perfect spider web, decked with pearly dew drops, you have to admire the skill of the spider who made it.

A Spider Masterpiece For Your Wall

Orb webs can be as beautiful as the finest lace. Did you know there's a way to take a web home and hang it on your wall?

What You Need:

a small spray can of black or
    white enamel
newspaper
sheets of stiff paper or
    cardboard — black or white
    (use black paper with white
    enamel and white paper
    with black enamel)
a pair of scissors
a partner to work with

What to Do:

1. Choose a day when there is no wind. Go outdoors early in the morning, while the orb webs are fresh. Find a dry web in good condition.

2. ⊘ Now you are going to spray the web with enamel. You may need to ask your partner to hold up some newspaper behind the web. The newspaper will keep the

enamel from spraying on flowers, walls or other things. (Don't spray your partner by accident!)

3. ⊘ Keep the can about 60 cm (2 ft.) from the web while spraying. If you get too close, you might blow a hole in the web. Spray the web gently on both sides. The strands of the web will now be very sticky.

4. Now you have to place the paper against the web. It might be easier if you hold one edge of the paper and your partner holds the other. Try to keep the paper flat and touch all the strands of the web at the same time. The web will stick to the paper the second it touches, so you can't change your mind about how to place it.

5. Use the scissors to cut the strands from which the web is hanging.

6. You now have a beautiful web captured on your sheet of paper. Lay the paper flat to dry — this will take about 15 minutes. Don't touch the web while it's drying.

7. When the web is dry, you can cover it with a sheet of clear plastic wrap to protect it. You can frame your spider master-piece, or hang it on the wall just as it is. Now you can enjoy the web's beauty for a long time.

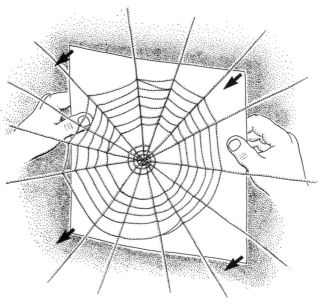

A Web Workshop

A spider will spin a web just for you, if you make a wood frame that the spider can use.

What You Need:

a large baking or roasting pan,
    at least 45 cm × 35 cm
    (18 in. × 14 in.)
some pieces of pine or other
    wood (see the drawing)
    2 pieces 50 cm (20 in.) long,
    for posts
    2 pieces 35 cm (14 in.) long,
    for cross rails
    2 pieces 20 cm (8 in.) long,
    for feet
nails
a spider that spins orb webs,
    such as a yellow and black
    garden spider

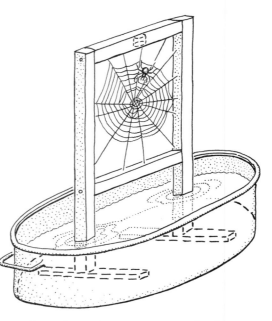

What to Do:

1. ⊘ Follow these steps to make a frame for a spider web. Nail the feet to the bottom of the posts. Nail the two crossrails to the posts. The drawing shows you what your frame should look like.

2. ⊘ Spiders like to have a place where they can hide. You might ask a grownup to drill a 1 cm (½ in.) hideout hole in the top crossrail.

3. Fill the large pan with water. Stand the frame in the water. The water will keep your spider from escaping.
4. Look outdoors for a spider that is spinning an orb web or sitting in the centre of one. Capture the spider in a jar and quickly put the lid on. Be patient — it may take a while to find the right spider.
5. Put the spider in the frame. It probably won't spin a web right away. Give your spider two or three days to get used to the frame. It will likely spin its web at night or in the early morning. On about the third or fourth morning, you should find an orb web spun inside the frame.

6. If you would like to keep the spider for a few more days, you will have to feed it. Capture some houseflies in a jar and throw them into the web. What does the spider do?
7. After about a week, let the spider go near the spot where you captured it.

Drop Me a Line

You can watch a spider let itself down on a rope of silk.

What You Need:

a spider
a pencil

What to Do:

1. Capture a spider. (Use the glass and cardboard method on page 11).
2. Let the spider walk onto a pencil. Hold the pencil at chest height, over an open patch of floor or sidewalk. *Gently* push the spider toward the end of the pencil. When it reaches the pointed tip, carefully push it off. What does the spider do?
3. How does the spider lower itself? Do any of its legs touch the silk strand?
4. Before the spider reaches the floor, touch it lightly. It will probably climb back up its strand. How many legs does it use to climb? What happens to its silk line as it climbs up?
5. Try this with different kinds of spiders. When you are finished, let the spiders go where you found them.

A Surprising Use For A Bubble

All spiders breathe air, just as you do. But the water spider lives its whole life underwater . How does the spider do it? It spins a small web underwater and attaches the web to a water weed. Then the spider rises to the surface of the water. It kicks its legs. A small bubble of air is trapped against its abdomen. The spider swims back down into the water and attaches the air bubble to its web. Up and down the spider goes, and on each trip it collects a little air bubble. Each new bubble combines with those already attached to the web. They join to make one air bubble that gets bigger and bigger. When it is big enough, the spider moves into its bubble home. Now it has all the air it needs — and a big window too!

Spiders in Space

Who were the first spidernauts? They were two orb web spiders nick-named Arabella and Anita. They were taken up in the Skylab to see if they could spin webs in space. In space there is no gravity — the force that holds us on the earth. Scientists thought that without gravity, Arabella and Anita might not be able to make their webs. They did, though. Their webs were just not as neat as they would be on earth.

Bad News for Insects

Spiders made their first appearance on earth about 300 million years ago. This was about the time the first flying insects appeared. In fact, some people who study insects think they developed wings to try to get away from spiders! Today, there are about 23,000 different kinds of spiders. They're still eating insects in huge amounts. In fact, the weight of insects eaten by spiders each year is probably greater than the total weight of all the people living on earth.

The Truth About Tarantulas

People who make adventure movies know one sure way to give the audience a scare. They just show a tarantula spider scuttling across the hero or heroine. Tarantulas certainly look dangerous. Their bodies are big and hairy. With their legs stretched out, they can be 30 cm (12 inches) wide. When they are cornered, they rear up on their hind legs and make a hissing noise. But, in spite of all this, they are timid spiders who would rather hide than fight. Some people even keep tarantulas as pets. They have to be careful in handling them, though. This is not just because of their bite. (Tarantulas won't bite unless they feel threatened, and their bite causes no more pain and swelling than a bee sting.) It's because of their hairs, which brush off easily. They give some people a bad rash!

TARANTULA

Index